PROPER ETIQUETTE IN THE SLAUGHTERHOUSE LINE

Poems by James H Duncan

GUTTER SNOB BOOKS

Proper Etiquette in the Slaughterhouse Line
Copyright ©2022 JAMES H DUNCAN
ISBN: 979-8-9858223-2-8

All rights reserved. Printed in the United States of America. No part of this text may be used or reproduced in any manner without written permission from the author or publisher except in the case of brief quotations embodied in critical articles and reviews.

Editor: Michele McDannold

Gutter Snob Books
200 W. Main St.
Trinidad, Colorado 81082

CONTENTS

Lunch Break	1
The Work We Do	3
proper etiquette in the slaughterhouse line	5
Standards of Quality	7
Don't Say I Didn't Warn You	12
Park Avenue	14
soft white infinity	15
Revenant	18
A Case of the Mondays	20
The Cold Northern Edge of Your Rope	23
Dance and Rattle	25
At the End of All Things	27
Feast	29
A small hymn for whoever comes next	31
Express Train Immolation	33
Texas Pacific	35
Through the Long Dark Night Alone	37
Bio	40
ACKNOWLEDGEMENTS	42

Lunch Break

there is an inbox mounted on the wall

at the end of the hallway outside

the executive editor's office,

and during each monthly meeting

she reminds us all

that it is full of resumes

    —I CAN REPLACE ANY OF YOU,

she says, WITH ONE PHONE CALL

the hillside rising from the edge of the parking

lot is overgrown with wildflowers

and sometimes I take my lunch break there,

sit in my car and watch the tall weeds,

flowers, and grass sway in the wind, and

it reminds me of an old Steinbeck novel I can't

recall, the one where those

  hobos and workers are hiding beneath

a bridge talking about their lives, their work,

escape, empowerment

the people here, they cannot escape;

  they have children and debt to consider,

husbands and wives and good things and bad
things holding them accountable
and rooted to this place, held so strong that
ideology and impractical wonderments
cannot move them, only catastrophe

I finish my sandwich and watch the hillside
full of flowers and tall grass move in the sun

there is a meeting at 1:30 and a 4 p.m. deadline,
  so I leave my sandwich wrapper in a ball
on the passenger seat slowly uncoiling itself
in the sun as I go back inside and wait
for catastrophe, or something much worse

The Work We Do

the work we do, all of us,

this whole universe of spreadsheets

and emails and wrenches and

lesson plans and bus routes,

this work we do is just to keep

us from thinking of Love

waking up and knowing

you're not there but smelling you,

still having to put on shoes and

drive through steel and anger

to reply to meeting invitations

and restock the shelves

and create department budgets

and replace the alternator in

someone's Toyota, or even call back

some child's mother who demands

to know why this life isn't what

she thought it would be for her child

as snow falls outside our collective

office windows

nothing is what we think it will be
no matter how we try, and
nothing will keep me from thinking of
the smell of your shampoo
or the way your hair falls across
your face when you fall asleep reading
—no matter how many times they
stand before us at a podium to declare
"We Are All One Big Family Here"
before casting us to the salt mines,
I think of you, I think of you like that

so as I reach over and turn out
the light for you and settle into bed,
know I am always looking for a way out
as we all pretend this isn't a maze that only
leads to a sluice, a darkness, a room where
we are put to work to stop thinking about
Love and the singular hope of holding
your hand to the very end

PROPER ETIQUETTE IN THE SLAUGHTERHOUSE LINE

it is never polite to stand on the bus bench
and claw at the red lights humming down
from the traffic signal like the fevered
eyes of the man in the moon whistling
along the astral highway to the inevitable
end of the road, end of the tracks, total night

citizens frown upon dashing empty beer bottles
against the grain of their blind shuffle home,
toward second jobs, toward the café turned bar
turned the lights out and now the streets are
empty save for footsteps from some drunk
walking 'round waking everyone up with his
constant daydreaming in the shade of his heart

he cries into those broken shards spread out
across our prairies and our playgrounds
across the oil-slicked cemeteries where our
luckiest bones might become petroleum
fueling even greater wars for water, for blood,
for country—no, for a man who waves a flag
from a balcony on fire, smiles all around

but in this dark night by the bus bench, the cats
   don't care much for pain or faith, and don't stare
unless there something worth staring at, so inhuman
   in that way, so much more human in most other ways,
slowing their pulse, slimming their eyes, breathing
   once an hour as the moon slides into the distant shore
to find the dust motes of our lost days and nights

   days of hunger, nights of thirst, all of us stifling
our moans and wailing in our own special way,
   hiding the fear and total understanding that there all
these rules we follow on the way to death that don't
   make sense, but we follow them every day, in every way,
taking care to ignore the crying drunk, proper etiquette,
like cattle into an empty factory lit by the ghost of the sun

Standards of Quality

I missed the call from HR while
vomiting blood in the bathroom, holding
my weight against the porcelain sink

my reflection shakes
in the mirror, looking for all
the world like those animals
they show in the ASPCA
commercials, and it takes another
half-hour to get myself back
to my desk of scattered Post-its
with reminders about meds,
appointments at Sloan Kettering,
reminders of deadlines for books
no one will buy or read in three years
time, rubber bands, Bic pens,
a flashing light on the phone

through a pharmaceutical fog
I remember a speech some
economist gave at my college
graduation, something about
owning your future

well, it takes me four times
to get the code right
for the voicemail
because my memory
is shot through like
the bloated pink body
on that Operation game
from my childhood
and each mistake
I make is that god
damned buzzer going off
grinding me down
just a little more

orange medicine bottles
take two pills twice a day
apply as needed
no more than eight every
24 hours, may cause
drowsiness, may cause
blindness, may cause
heart palpitations, may cause…

I finally get through to find
HR has made their decision

and they appreciate the struggle
I have gone through
over the last six months
but I just don't meet
the company's standards of
quality at this time

I can almost see them
at the conference table out
there in Illinois, the pine
trees just outside that massive
floor-to-ceiling window,
all of them looking at each other
waiting awkwardly for my
response, bitter at the drawn out
process, bitter at having to
recognize the cog for what it is

if I am a cog I am
chipped teeth spinning wild
unable to hold the rhythm of
dawn-to-dusk drop-down
menus and bottom-line consistency,
not anymore

COBRA says I can keep my
insurance but the rates are higher
than all of my utilities combined
and I wonder how long I can
go without power, without AC,
maybe recharge phones and laptops
at local cafes and shower cold and hold
on until autumn when the temps drop
back to humane levels, but I know
it's too much, too much, wandering the
radiated streets of summer, just
too much to handle in the haze of
cancer and debt and my cell phone
buzzing at another lawyer's threats

but I keep walking, I keep
wiping away the blood from my
chin, from my clothing and hair

I keep rising in the morning,
I keep fighting when HR
drops my insurance anyway

I keep arguing with Blue Shield,
Medicaid, Social Security, the people

at the unemployment office, the landlord,
ConEd, Time Warner, the DMV, the
secretaries at the hospital and the labs,
with the voice in my own head telling me
it's not worth it anymore

then I feel my friend's hand slip
into mine across the dinner table
and another falls in step with me
as I walk across the Pulaski Bridge
where the sunset burns rose gold down
every street and despite the
blood on my bedsheets and the
crying in the bathroom every night
I see that, somehow, a lush green foliage
erupts out of this salted earth
rising all around me, telling me it is
still possible to ascend through the shit
it is still possible to feel the sun on my face

as the cogs keep spinning, burning towards
standards of quality I'll never know

Don't Say I Didn't Warn You

there are cracks forming
in the shell of this world,
forming in our sleep, and
we don't always see them
when we wake, when we
work, when we try to love
and hurry and hustle until
we glance up, pause, and
there they are, the hairline
fractures along the ceiling,
little sutures in the walls,
the house lilting just a bit,
barely visible if you look
hard enough—but, hey,
it's fine, everything will
be fine, right? if we just
leave it like that? there's no
emergency, it seems to be
holding itself upright just
fine, and the Tower of Pisa
has been that way for age
upon age, so who's worried

about one more filament of
space and time broken away
to graveyard dust? so let the
cash roll in as we look away,
and look away further, and
soon we'll leave that house
for another one, a better one,
a place with white walls and
good Thai food nearby, better
WiFi and that casual sense of
suburban anonymity, just one
more animal avoiding total
extinction until the chain of
command somewhere overhead
loses link after link, crack after
crack, and the tide begins to lap
at our ankles, standing on the peak
of the world, holding our iPhone 25
up to the sky, begging for help as
the satellites pass us by, glimmering
amongst the garbage and stars above
until even they melt in the brilliant
embrace of an unforgiving sun

Park Avenue

waiting at the crosswalk I encountered

a large dog on a leash, russet-blonde hair

all shaggy with great brown glistening eyes,

he looked at me and I looked at him

and we understood each other

in ways that I haven't felt understood in weeks,

and his owner

tugged on his leash and he turned away

looking back only once among

the taxis, ear-buds, Italian shoes,

the constant heart-shaking rattle of NYC

and he knew, and I knew

and I walked back to my office where I ate

my food and drank my water and laid down

my head in my little designated

space and began to wait for whatever

came next

SOFT WHITE INFINITY

snow comes down through the trees
in slow motion, weaving between
thin twisted bones of sleeping oaks,
elms, maples, a stunted white birch,
haphazard vectors of nuclear winter
fulfilling a promise, a silent promise

the peacefulness of the scene is
almost enough to make the hell of
human greed and vitriol disappear

it's almost enough to make the ruddy
American face of smiling cruelty fade
to soft white infinity of a silent earth

people fear the young who protest
people fear the rich who bloviate
people fear the end of the world
because it is the end of *their* world
but a million silent forests with nothing
but sleeping oaks, elms, maples, a stunted
white birch, a kingdom far greater than

any heavenly triumph or biblical lie

as Kerouac said, "one man practicing
kindness in the wilderness is worth
all the temples this world pulls"

the only greater thing is a wilderness
with no Man at all, no cell tower humming
sending off hashtags and useless videos

in the simplest of terms, we are not great
enough to warrant infinity

in the simplest of terms, our end
is but a single snowflake falling so
slowly through the bones of the trees,
and we may fight and uphold all
that is good and just, but in time, evil
will gather up in its arms
all its wealthy possessions
and press the red button out of spite

don't let this make you sad
or lose sight of the goodness you possess

if you're going to die, die with decency
and remember—
white snowflakes will fall
and have always fallen,
and fall even now

no matter what else may befall
this humanity, this Earth,
that truth will remain forever

Revenant

the third missed call is indicated
by a flashing green light

you pick it up just as a snowplow truck
grattles and roughs its way past the house

up County Route 150, and you wonder who else
is out on those roads so late, after so
much of the world gave up and went home
to ride out the worst of it

and yet

the night and the snow falls harder than ever

the electric heater along the baseboard
ticks madly, then the door downstairs closes

footfalls on the steps, rising

you move to the kitchen to watch
the apartment's front door

phone in hand, the green light
no longer flashing

no longer alone

A Case of the Mondays

it is 4:30 a.m. and dawn is
somewhere—but not here

sirens came through the night and
the curtains, but now—silence

they say they'll pay us double
they say they'll pay us triple
they keep the lights on and
the registers open, they keep
the time clocks ticking even
though the world clocks are
grinding to a halt on every
continent around the globe

it is 4:45 a.m. and dawn is
not coming—not anymore

of course, the sun will rise but
that isn't the same thing, is it?

they say the stock market crash is

good for us, it will help, like they
said the stock market soaring was
good nine months ago—it's all
bedtime stories told by men in
ties who don't know anything
about anything worthwhile now,
but they say Wall Street is open
even though Main Street is dead

it is 5:09 a.m. and dawn is the glow
of distant fires on the horizon

you pick up your phone but there is no
society found in those wires anymore

your work badge and the last of your
sandwich meat in the last of your bread
waits in your work bag by the door, as
smoke fills the sky, blurring the neighbor's
American flag and red political lawn signs

that neighbor hasn't come outside in days
that neighbor will never come outside again

it is 6:30 a.m. and you hope the end
will be quick, but you also know better

you rise; you open the door to another shift on
Earth,
the monetization of your soul relentless and
unending

and disappear
into the fog

THE COLD NORTHERN EDGE OF YOUR ROPE

she whispers to turn off the radio,
the small black receiver on the nightstand
softly humming the news of the day:
another front in the war, another school
littered with shell casings and blood,
another ending before it could begin;
she reaches over me and turns the dial
to soft static like an ocean breeze
parting the sheer curtains that now dance
across the room, linen white and cool

inchoate peace, drifting dreams;
if we burrow down into the forgiving dawn
it may be possible to hold on to the days
that came before the end of all things,
before loading the car at night
and driving with no headlights,
before wishing coworkers a good
weekend but knowing you'd never
see them again, hoping they make it

nobody will make it, you ponder

as her warm arm slips over your back
and you feel lucky to be so far from
the end before it comes, and maybe
it won't ever come, maybe the fire
will burn itself out before it reaches
the cold northern edge of your rope
where you hang and swing and wait
in this forest retreat, blue skies, cold
dreams, and that whispering radio

but you look at the radio, and you know

our strength is our ability to deceive:
others if we can, ourselves most of all;
we have for too long now, and now
as the curtains dance in the light and her
warm arm slips across your back
you hope you can pull the trick again
for just a little while more

before ash turns to ash once again

Dance and Rattle

they scream, the billows of wind
through the trees and the reeds and
the glens throughout the uncollected
beauty of this wilderness, they scream,
the air seething through the thinnest
reaches of the trees and leaves, white
pop of light beyond the horizon while
here the birds sing, then pause before
they too scream

lichen and a gentle stream wending
through the ancient stone and earthen
paths that lead deeper, further away,
but the wind has that smell now, and
on the rocky outcrop my bones sense
the change in the weather; cells molt
and reel and vibrate with molecular
dissonance; though it is quiet now I
think they too will scream before long

yes, quiet—the reeds have even stopped
their dance and rattle, the birds like small

black commas along the ground, little
feet clawing at the sky as the world turns
on an unseen/unfelt axis, as it always has
and always will, with or without us

this outcropping with a view of the valley
is a fine place to see our final ending,
silent and stoic as the earth has
always been, and I too have become
a disciple of this silence,
my blood screaming through veins,
down into the mottled cracks of
stone and lichen, a gentle stream,
then one final sudden flash of white
in the distance, mass molecular implosions
and then I'm safe at last

At the End of All Things

prepared against failure, we fail

the reserves of water in the camel pack
are sucked through the hose
to the mouth and spat to the ground,
the water tainted, rancid
with amorphous disease,
the very source of life, *death*

stooping at the crossroads creek, the freshest
tendrils in a land of spoil—gray water
pours out onto the gravel road and clear runoff
fills the bag, but the illness and taste
of rot remains, like the hideous hope that the others
along the trail hold in their faith, their heroes,
their systems of human profit and order,
just a bad taste, a stain that lingers
until the bones shudder and fail

along the trail there are bones and shoes, but
the possibility of tainted clear water is
a better kind of hope than tainted sludge, in the

same way you hold to the delusion that

the next highway will not smolder,

that the next skyline fire will not be yours,

and you prepare your mind that way, drinking

clear water, taking the next step, working on luck,

leaning on the shoulder of your own broken mind,

preparing for failure, even as you fail

you keep going, just keep going

Feast

mastication takes hold long after dusk
when politics and biometrics no longer
matter, when the dogs have taken to
the fields and run from the walking bones
that stagger after, knives and claws working
in the ash-grey hollows of their eyes

dogs run wild through forests and wait
for the encampments to fall silent,
for bodies in tents and truck beds
to stop shifting, for the meat to pucker
against bone, and maybe then, when
the dogs that run wild grow hungry
enough, they might return to masticate
before escaping to the wasteland,
the purest form of aberration

through field and town, burning city after
burning city, Satan walking the ashen road,
looking at what we've done to ourselves
reading signs painted by finger, by blood,
clarity made complete through human

chaos and blundering—the meal has begun
and we are devouring ourselves to the
bone with every passing pettiness

the cruel truth is this:
no one stops eating once they begin,
not until there's nothing left
and the wind carries the sound of dogs
hungry for their share
across the purple mountain majesties
where true freedom unspoken
now reigns in charred peace and silence

A SMALL HYMN FOR WHOEVER COMES NEXT

bury those you find along the wooded path
and say a small prayer to the salt in the sea
and the dust hovering across our galaxy;

we were fools to believe in anything else,
the many mythologies and monetized
gospels of our collective youth now
collapsed into the one simple somnolent
truth as cold and pure as the crystalline
snow that will fall over our bones and boots
and assorted highway detritus, gifts from
a former age to grant us one last bonfire,
one last hand held in the night, one last
kiss before we crawl into the abandoned
shells of domesticity and faith—lies from those
great economic strawmen; there we will hold
each other until the sun goes black and our
bones entwine with whatever green world may
arise from our irradiated ash and desolation

if only we could see,
if only we could know

this world will become so beautiful,
if only for its lack of us

Express Train Immolation

the subway headlights gleam
against the black
steel
girders
as it pulls
through
the station,
past the pillars one by one
like a lantern running through hell
chasing after dawn

doors close and jerk forward // the car
is nearly empty // an ominous murmur
trickles through the midnight speakers
from some microphone left on by
a long gone conductor // whispers from
fifteen, twenty, or thirty years ago still
trickling
down
through
the wires

like dead radio prayers
come true

and somewhere above,
topside,
everything is dust and rubble

humanity lives by humanity's rules,
supposedly unbreakable, and when
they fall apart, what prevails?

ribbons of time and light // ghost
trains racing to hell in the night

whatever they decide to call *the end*,
they should realize that down here,
the rats still gnaw on refuse
the roaches still march
the pain of a flickering light
still lingers as station by station flies by:
empty platforms, holiday echoes, dimming
lanterns,
our bones rushing headlong into the universe
without us, content as ever

Texas Pacific

towns stand silent in western

gothic rust,

abandoned gas stations

in the distance hasten shadows,

obscure scrubland,

crawling darkness,

urging us onward, the divisor haunting

the memory of Satan drying

on the cross, rotting corpses finding

us at occasional intersections

and railroad crossings

the train lurches on,

each of us holding tight to the stupid

hope that all we've seen hasn't

reached ahead of us

to tarnish wherever waits

at the end of this line

I think of how April windows would

marble with sudden rain,

how the sun once broke free

during the heaviest
downfall in that small New England
town, every particle a diamond then,
every breath fresh with green and
blue procrastination,

but now it is all black,
no stars in the desert sky of western
Texas, an indolent remainder
of how it all began,
of how much we lost,
of a story that took too long to tell

the epilogue will not be kind, either

Through the Long Dark Night Alone

into the cold arms of the future, I go
stripped raw, bare nerves and bone
one stump placed before the other into the
snow and the dead leaves, through cities
fallen and homes decayed to rot, onward
into the cold arms of the future, I go
to find a home for you

this world will hurricane rage against your
innocence,
it will throw up every razor-wire hatred in your path,
and for all we did we deserve it, but if you
follow this way through the trees,
through the ravines, the badlands,
the long dark night ahead,
you may find the place where I fell,
maybe by the water's edge or in an open field
of tall grass and wildflowers
or maybe decomposing in the gray hardscrabble
of industrial carnage and rust,
unblinking eyes aching for the horizon

but when you find that place,
wherever I stopped,
keep going

there will be others behind you
following your slips and your stumbles,
watching for your footfall in the snow,
and one day they may catch up to you
or someone will to them,
or someone to them,
one of us will get there, one of us will make it
through dead leaves and rot,
beyond the barbed-wire and fire,
somewhere better, a place we haven't ruined,
and they will sit at last and rest,
perhaps wondering how they got there
or maybe they will wake as a child in that place
and know nothing but peace

that will be the reason
to place one stump before another
through the long dark night alone

if only for you

if only for you

and the peace I hope you'll find

when you get there

JAMES H DUNCAN

James H Duncan is the editor of *Hobo Camp Review* and the author of *We Are All Terminal But This Exit Is Mine*, *Vacancy*, *Feral Kingdom*, and *Beyond the Wounded Horizon*, among other collections of poetry and fiction. A former editor with Writer's Digest Books and *American Artist* magazine, you can currently find him on the road looking for independent bookshops to review for his blog, The Bookshop Hunter. For more, visit www.jameshduncan.com.

Acknowledgements

Some of the poems included in this collection were previously published in the following publications. Gutter Snob Books wishes to acknowledge these presses for their fine work and dedication to the small press.

"Texas Pacific" appeared in *Nixes Mate Review*

"The Cold Northern Edge of Your Rope" appeared in *Open Skies Quarterly*

"Soft White Infinity," "Feast," and "Don't Say I Didn't Warn You"
appeared in *Winedrunk Sidewalk*

MORE GUTTER SNOB BOOKS

SpaceTime Continuum for Dummies
Michele McDannold

Noise: art and words
Misti Rainwater-Lites

Marilyn: Self-Portrait, Oil on Canvas
Kerry Trautman

Running Red Lights
Aleathia Drehmer

Satan's Kiss
Alan Catlin

Texaz Bluez
Catfish McDaris

Made in the USA
Middletown, DE
01 May 2022

64969676R00031